Focused, Unstuck and Back in Action

THE SECRETS FOR HAPPINESS

AND IMPROVING YOUR LIFE

NO MATTER WHAT!

MYRA GOLDICK

Published by:
Living Through Art, Inc.

DEDICATION

I wrote this book in loving memory of both my mother and father who brought me into this glorious world.

I dedicate this workbook to my loving husband Neil, and my two daughters, Karen and Janine. Their support and faith in me has made it possible to follow my dreams and goals. Their unyielding belief and recognition of my efforts have helped make my journey through life a fruitful one..

CONTENTS

Happiness IS waiting for you!

Life is often challenging and isolated. We all have our own personal struggles and adversities. One thing which is ignored and overlooked throughout time is the simple fact that those of us who have traveled through the darkness can offer help to others as they struggle to find the light of self-fulfillment.

I believe no one has to be alone on that dark and lonely journey. Personal experience has taught me that sharing, compassion and understanding is a key that can unlock what may seem insurmountable odds and circumstantial entrapment.

To all who perceive themselves lost in a world of procrastination, indecision, and frustration, know that freedom and happiness are waiting for you.

INTRODUCTION
Focused, Unstuck, and BACK IN ACTION

Are you stuck? Are you dragging yourself through the hours between sunrise and sunset in survival mode, moving from one task to another without joy or passion, struggling to find meaning or purpose in your life? You know it's there somewhere, buried behind the negative words. Like a fair-weather friend, joie de vivre that makes life worth living, but it seems here today and gone tomorrow, and you're just wondering what it takes to bring it back into your life.

Maybe you had it once but misplaced it, and even though you've been searching high and low, your motivation is nowhere to be found.

Maybe, like me, you began your life behind the proverbial eight-ball, and what you really need is a clue, just one clue that will help you find the path that will take you to loving yourself, loving your life, and unlocking your passion.

Wherever you began, however far you have come, right now you feel stuck. And more than anything you want to get unstuck, focused, and back in action, but how? All roads, whether long or short, begin with a single step, but where do you start? You start here. With my help, you can begin to turn your depression and sadness into joy. I promise!

Within these pages I will share the key I use to restart my engine when life grinds me to a halt. The exercises in the Focused, Unstuck and Back in Action helped me create a life for myself, despite the poverty I was born into and the disease I was attacked by. In spite of very poor choices and extreme self-loathing, I was able to use these exercises to turn my life on – gifting myself with direction, achievement, and the love I learned I deserved.

Many times over the years, in the face of numerous difficulties, I have come back to this practice. Without fail, it sets my mind in the right direction and leads me from stuck, unfocused, and out of action back to unstuck, focused, , and back in action – right where I really want to be.

We begin with introspection. After all, unless you know yourself and take the time to tune in to the things that fill you with the desire to move, explore, and create, how can you have passion for life?

Without passion, how can you have direction? I'm talking about the kind of direction that comes from inside you. How do you know which way to turn and put one foot in front of the other - to go from stuck to unstuck if you have no idea where your passion lies? It is when you gain insight about yourself that you can then move forward, one step at a time. This workbook is your first step.

Being "stuck" takes a toll on mind, spirit, and body. I am sharing a key that opens the door to a different world, where being stuck is temporary and getting unstuck allows you to reinvent yourself whenever and however you choose. How quickly that door appears and how well that key works is up to you. The same key can turn your life on, as it did for me. Be forewarned: As with most aspects of life, the results are equal to the effort.

Trust me, I speak from experience. My life changed when I put in the mental and emotional effort required of me. My depression turned to joy and I embraced my passion, took it seriously, and let it lead me into a life where I
positively thrived. With this transformation came a second passion: Reaching out to others who are stuck in self-destructive patterns, to offer my experience and insight, and to help them find a way back to a life of abundant joy.

Today, I am a motivational speaker, author, disability advocate, professional artist, wife, mother, and grandmother. I host two online radio shows, Never Say Impossible and Dancing On Our Disabilities, which   can   be   accessed   at   Talkshoe.com http://www.talkshoe.com/tc/126304 and on my website as well at http://myragoldick.com on the show archive page. My prior professional experience included a 20-year career in sales and marketing in the corporate cosmetic industry and 8 more in the fashion design Industry on 7th Avenue in New York City.

None of these achievements seemed possible in my formative years. Statistically, when, where, and how I started my life should have led to completely different results. However, along with everything it threw at me, life also gave me the opportunity to learn the power of the words "Never Say Impossible" at an early age, when I needed them the most. They have been my mantra since the very beginning of the hardest fight of my life.

If anyone knows about reinventing themselves in the face of adversity, it's me. In this book I am going to share a little of my story with the hope that it will inspire you to say to yourself, "Well. If she can do it, so can I!"

You are also going to get plenty of powerful exercises that are going to move you from being stuck to living your life with joy, happiness and purpose. Are you ready? Let's get started!

Note: **Please have paper and a pen nearby to write down your answers to the exercises. This will make the exercises more effective and you will have record of your thoughts and feeling**

CHAPTER ONE:
Everyone Has a Story

Learning what other people experience in their life's can be eye opening. Sharing your own story with others reminds us that we are not alone in our joys, or in our disappointments. Sharing our wins is fun and it inspirers the others to think in a positive manor and believe that they too can create great things in their own world. It does not stop there. How about sharing the not so good stuff? Some events are so unexpected and devastating they stop us in our tracks and leave us feeling vulnerable. Admitting our disappointments can fore-warn others, while at the same time liberating us. We all go through transitions and we have all made mistakes. An essential component for getting back in action is learning how others have overcome adversity and challenges and just as importantly how they bring joy back into their lives.

This is my story

I was born in New York City during World War II. My mother was Austrian, my father was Trinidadian, and I was a mixed-race child in a time when the color of my skin was a strike against me.

My parents separated when I was six years old, which was just another bump in a childhood filled with turmoil. When I say I started life behind the eight ball, I mean my mother, brother, and I were a little family tossed about on a very stormy sea of domestic violence, alcoholism, hunger, single-room-occupancies, homelessness, and poverty.

I remember being awakened in the night - more than once - and ordered to grab what I could carry so that we could run off in the dark to avoid another unpaid landlord would miss us. Leaving my personal belongings behind was a way of life. Birthday and Christmas presents that were stolen from us by my father during the night as we were sleeping, to be sold for money, was also a way of life.

Add to that racial discrimination, constant moving from one single room occupancy to another, bullying, and hand-me-down clothing from charities, loss of innocence, isolation and loneliness, and I'm sure you can imagine how difficult it was to nurture any sense of self-esteem.

My father was a musician with a career in decline. Money was earned sporadically, and he came in and out of our lives just as unpredictably, bringing promises when he showed up but leaving heartache in his wake.

My mother, humbled by dependence on welfare, was steadfast in her values, and very strict. It was for our protection. We spent many nights in dangerous places, and often my only options for friends were the sad, unfortunate addicts and losers who lived around us, as well as their children. I was rarely allowed to play with others, let alone develop friendships.

Sadly, those were the best years of my childhood.

Part of me thought this life was normal - painful, but normal. Another part of me thought there must be something better. I hung on stubbornly to the belief that there had to be a better life somewhere, maybe in the future.

Like many children, I escaped reality with dreams of growing up and going out into a different world. My greatest fantasy was becoming a glamorous dancer who dazzled on stage and was admired by audiences far and wide. That represented love to me in my childish analysis of what acceptance meant.

Magically, I discovered that between pretending to be a Broadway star and remembering where I really was, I could shut out the ugliness around me when I put my crayons to good use.

From an early age, I chose to make friends with my coloring books and crayons. I used them to try to create a world that was filled with joy, laughter, bright colors, and a sense of freedom and belonging instead of tears, anger, gloom, bullying and rejection.

Creativity became my salvation. I felt alive in the quiet time spent trying to recreate the brilliance of nature's colors. Using my childhood creativity as a survival tool, I placed my own image in every drawing filled with the joy of breathtaking color. Art became the joy in my little life, and although I had no idea at the time, creativity would end up saving my life many times over.

Stop for a moment. Examine where you believe your creativity lies. We all are innately gifted in unique areas. Where are your talents? Write down the first five things that pop into your mind.

...And then, things got worse.

At the age of ten I was attacked by one of the most dreaded childhood diseases of the 20th century: Polio. It paralyzed my little body completely, and utterly trapping me inside myself.

It happened suddenly. I remember shopping at a thrift store with my father in the afternoon, then going to bed with a fever that night. Ten dayslater, I awakened from a coma - to the surprise of a room full of doctors and nurses who thought I was going to die instead.

Even though I lived, what happened to me was its own kind of torturous death. The virus ravaged me, leaving extensive nerve damage in its wake. My physical, muscular, and skeletal forms were changed forever.

Worse than the changes that could be seen were the changes that were hidden in my psyche. My identity took a beating. The self-esteem that had only just begun to bud through my art was squashed under the foot of disease.

I was screaming in my head, flailing against my frozen limbs. You may have heard the expression, "The spirit is willing but the flesh is weak," but unless you have been trapped inside a body that refuses to obey any of your commands, you can only guess at what that really means.

I questioned my future and what was in store for me. The awful "what if" scenarios kept running through my head. When I heard something negative from any of the various caregivers who were attending to my broken body, I would begin to nose dive emotionally and lose all hope and faith.

There are no words to describe how painful my own negative self talk and fears were. Just as I was letting my feelings get crushed under the weight of my own fears, I changed my mind about all my possibilities and about what was in store for me. I refused to listen to anyone else's thought about what I could achieve. I decided then and there that the negative opinions of others were totally and completely unacceptable.

Even at that delicate age, as I lay on my recovery bed in the middle of a rundown, infectious disease hospital, unable to move one single muscle, I knew that there was no way I could accept anyone else's limited opinion of my potential.

Slowly, painfully, I began a long, eight-year battle to rebuild my body. I learned to walk again. I regained my independence. I retrained the muscles in my hands so I could draw and create colorful worlds on paper again.

Polio isolated me more than poverty had ever done. Learning to walk and draw and control my movements again ate up my teen years. It swallowed them whole.

I can honestly tell you the braces, crutches, and wheelchairs, and the years of rehabilitation, painful surgeries and exercise were far easier to endure than the mental and emotional challenges that lay ahead. I had to build self-esteem from nothing, whip up self-confidence from nowhere, and accept with no nonsense that some dreams, like dancing, would have to be replaced by new ones.

Letting go of a dream because you have come to the conclusion that it is not actually for you is very different from having that dream yanked out from under your feet by a disease that refuses to even let you try. Without my permission, the ravages of polio stole my dream of becoming a dancer, and with it a child's concept of freedom and acceptance.

It almost stole my ability to exercise my passion for art, but without creativity my life would lose its light so I found a way to teach my muscles to hold a crayon. I had to remember what it was like before the paralysis, when drawing, coloring and painting were done with ease. Relearning to make that crayon move and leave a controlled mark was a major challenge. Once I learned to control the crayons, those marks began once again to represent what I was feeling deep within my heart.

I spent the first three years of recovery dividing my time between intense physical therapy and home instruction schooling. The Board of Education provided once per week home instruction. I learned to walk again with the aid of crutches and braces and returned to school at the tender and vulnerable age of 13.

Do you remember 13? Do you remember the changes your body was going through, the fickle nature of your friends, budding romances, slumber parties, school dances, PE classes, and why a crush is called a crush? Thirteen is when I transitioned back into a real school and back into a world of cruel teenagers and heartless bullies.

When circumstances happen *to you* instead of *because of you*, and steal something of your soul without your permission, it is very easy to become stuck. More than a temporary rut, being stuck in old mindsets can be almost as paralyzing as polio. I speak from experience.

My story is full of extreme examples. I bring them out in the open to give hope to those of you who think you are alone in the difficulty of your challenges. None of us are alone and no odds are insurmountable.

I would like you to understand that soul-crushing events and negative conditioning can come in many sizes and many packages, with many disguises and many ways to inflict pain. I want you to take this moment to pause and acknowledge that whatever has made you stuck, big or small, is a big deal. Healing it is worth your time and attention, no matter how much work goes into it. You are worth your time and attention.

Be gentle in your judgment. What seems like a walk in the park to your neighbor may be burying you alive? The apparent size of the trauma has little to do with how much room it takes up in your psyche. If you are facing a challenge of any kind that is holding you back, and it paralyzes you figuratively, it is just as significant and important to heal as if it were paralyzing you literally.

While you read my story, keep in mind that in spite of it all, I created a wonderful life of abundance for myself. People think I created it from thin air, but in reality, I created it from the solid stuff I found inside myself when I learned where to look. INWARD!

What's next?

When your dreams die, grieving your losses is only natural.

Physical struggle and limitation ate up my entire teenage years, from puberty through young adulthood. Inside, I was just like any other girl, self-conscious of physical changes, eager for acceptance, lost in love songs, and fantasizing about boys and boyfriends. On the outside, my body refused to cooperate.

What I saw in the mirror was not what I envisioned in my mind. I was confronted by an image I hated, the reflection of a body that had been changed by a disease that had left its mark on my skeletal form and my muscles. I gained 50 pounds in one year. I was growing into a teenager who felt uglier on the inside than I thought I looked on the outside, if that was possible.

I was unable to imagine there was anything of value inside me. I may have been tough enough to rebuild my body, but beyond that I was a fragile, damaged little girl inside with no sense of her beauty, value, or place in the world.

Like many of us, I was able to cope with life and school on the outside, but I was drowning in insecurity and fear on the inside. Maybe you succeed at work, or accomplish great things as a parent or leader in the community, but inside something is sticking against itself. I knew I needed to change what was going on inside, but how to make that change was a baffling mystery.

Is this at all familiar?

I spent the next four years perfecting my physical appearance, but neglecting my inner spirit. I wore crazy makeup and wild hairstyles like a mask. I turned boring, cheap clothes into dramatic costumes just to draw attention. I believed in my costuming, which had nothing to do with believing in myself.

What is your costume? Could it be clothing, cars, or a cul-de-sac address? Or maybe it's tattoos, piercings, or wild hair? Perhaps you wrap yourself in politics, religion, or service? All of these things are fine, and even joyful, as long as they are genuine to you sincerely are. If they are worn to hide who you really are, the mask is adding to your problem.

I was trying to disguise myself and drown out my own self-talk – you know, the inner voice that loves to tell you you're a fake and a failure and you're fooling no one? That voice is a liar, but boy is it loud sometimes.

My inner voice was such a liar, it had me convinced that I deserved the polio and all its pain and all its damage. Have you ever met a child of 10 who "deserved" any such thing?

It was so bad and so persuasive that I allowed myself to be abused by others, and I abused myself. I settled for bad boyfriends and associations with losers. I could say I was only looking for what I expected from life, but as I said before, somewhere deep inside I knew there was a much better way to live.

I struggled through those years trying to remind myself of the faith and courage I had held onto when I survived polio. It was slipping away. I questioned my faith in myself. The isolation and depression were overwhelming. All my childhood dark years, combined, those events doubled and tripled the weight of my pile of "evidence" that I was completely worthless.

Sink or swim: now what?

I tried to take my life. Again, death evaded me. I began the daunting task of asking myself the painful questions, such as "Why am I so un-accepting of myself?"

I needed help. I could either continue to destroy myself, or I could find the strength to survive and to flourish. I was stuck and not going anywhere in my emotional life, so I threw myself into my art and school. I was determined to complete my senior year of high school with outstanding grades; that was one thing in my life I did feel I could control. It was up to me and I wanted to live and be happy.

That was the beginning of the best decision I have ever made for myself.

As a result of this renewed interest in school, an English teacher paid attention to my efforts and recognized my potential. She told me I could change my life significantly, if I was willing to do some creative thinking.

She became a life-coach of sorts, informally giving me advice and offering guidance here and there. I clung to it for dear life. I hung on to every word she generously shared with me, and let her encouraging voice begin to replace my nasty inner voice.

I will never forget one of the assignments she gave me. It changed my life – many times and in the face of many challenges. I have adapted it for this workbook, trusting that it will be just as valuable to you.

It was so simple and at the same time so difficult, but I stuck with it and learned the secret to becoming unstuck.

My first "unsticking" happened at the beginning of my senior year. How far could a simple assignment take someone? Well, this self-destructive, suicidal girl put the right time and attention into it and graduated from high school with a full scholarship to the prestigious Fashion Institute of Technology (FIT) in New York, where I began working towards a degree in Fashion Illustration. I was on a new path.

Becoming unstuck during my teenage years taught me a valuable, unforgettable life lesson. During my life I have hit roadblocks and felt "stuck" numerous times. Lessons learned last a lifetime. I always turned back to these exercises and began the life-saving practice of soul-searching self-examination, and inevitably I would free myself and become productive, happy, and successful again.

It's strange how one generous person who wants to offer assistance can change the way you think. As I began to regain my emotional stability, I once again began to practice the assignment, which my English teacher had gifted to me. It became my guiding light as I created a life of abundant joy. It became an exercise I would practice for the rest of my life whenever my spiritual self felt trapped and stuck.

I began with no direction and ended with a plan. I embarked on a career in cosmetic sales and marketing that lasted two decades. I was extremely successful, deeply satisfied, and strengthened every day by the act of doing something I loved and was very, very good at.

I met the man of my dreams, married him, and gave birth to his children – who are thriving. I built one career and then another, served my community, and lived a life full of light, laughter, friendship, love, and acceptance.

Life happens without our consent and things may change suddenly.

And then, Polio attacked a second time.

Post-Polio Syndrome hit me hard as an adult, forcing me out of my much-loved lucrative career and threatening to get me stuck all over again. I refused to let it destroy me; that would have been worse than death. Instead, I returned to these exercises and went through them diligently and faithfully. I discovered a new purpose within my sustaining passion. Each of the exercises renewed my motivation and drive.

I began a new chapter in my life just as exciting as the one that had just closed. I returned to the Fashion Institute of Technology and this time earned a degree in Millinery Design. My reward for returning to the exercises that had proven so helpful years ago was a new, thrilling, eight-year adventure designing millinery for some of the world's most renowned fashion designers on 7th Avenue in New York City.

Are you willing to begin to change your life today by getting unstuck?

I let it change my life - will you let it change yours?

CHAPTER TWO:
Who are you?
Preparation is the Key to Success

A few simple questions:

When you think of your childhood what do you feel? What emotions are evoked? Please be honest with yourself.

How about right now? Are you happy or unhappy?

Do you feel happy? It's a normal reaction to automatically smile spiritually when we feel or experience a happy emotion. When thinking of the past, memories often create beautiful pictures in our minds. What do you see right now? Is your mind painting joy filled images? Do you have positive expectations about the great things that tomorrow will bring your way?

Are you unhappy? If yes, it is important that you examine the source of your discontent. Is there something happening presently that creates a sense of frustration or disappointment? By pin pointing an event or events in your present life that are a source of unhappiness, you may discover that your unhappiness is linked back to an unresolved memory from the past. It is difficult to dismiss painful memories. We have a way of burying them deep within our minds. The bad news is that many hidden memories can appear spontaneously when external stimuli triggers us to react to something that reminds us of past events. Ask yourself if something you are experiencing currently is knocking on the door of negative memories?

Breaking it down into the three important areas

Most of us would agree there are three vitally important areas to develop in order to achieve success during and throughout life. These three areas are **Emotional** (which includes health), **Professional**, and **Financial**. Although it is possible to achieve success in one of those areas and not the other two, it is highly unlikely that without all three, you will feel fulfilled.

During my life's journey, I have discovered through introspection and observation, that letting go of old beliefs and self-destructive habits can be one of the most daunting tasks. I'm speaking about your pre-conceived opinions and beliefs of what you can or cannot achieve or simply what you believe you deserve to achieve. We begin to form habits and opinions very early in life. Those habits can prove to be very damaging. In fact, most of us would agree that by the time we've reached adolescence we have already begun to settle into habits and beliefs simply because we have been taught these habits, and they're in our comfort zone.

Breaking an old belief or habit takes work. That is the bad news. The good news is that we can all start over when we "get stuck." We can all do it and reinvent ourselves. I've done it over and over again, each time with great success. It might take a little work and a few mental exercises. However, if you take the time to prime yourself, you will see amazing results. Now it's time to examine yourself and figure out why you are feeling stuck.

Emotional

When you think about love, friendship, and health in your early life, what emotion do you feel?

Happy? Please explain why. Remember what happens to us in childhood remains with us throughout life.

Are you still feeling happy in your emotional life today or has something changed? Explain.

Please remember that we are examining your emotional life and the relationships that represent a sense of being loved or being able to return love.

It is important that you remain honest with yourself during these exercises.

Unhappy –Why? This will take some intense introspective questioning of your inner self.

Your happiness is up to you. Spiritual happiness cannot be gifted to you. External happiness is temporary and fleeting.

If you are unhappy, what would bring long lasting happiness into your life? Remember happiness is an inside job.

Do you feel your sense of wellbeing has been robbed from you through circumstances?

Has anything changed recently? Life happens without our consent.

What happened to create the uneasy feeling?

Now is the time to drag it out of the closet

Financial

When you think about money and finances in your childhood – What do you feel?

Secure - why? Did you have all your needs met?

Insecure - why? Do you remember feeling a lack of creature comforts? Did you secretly dream of abundance?

Professional

As a young person, what did you dream of doing when you became an adult?

Have you achieved that dream? Why isn't it still working?

Or did you shove it under the carpet or bed where it remains hidden from view? Why have you abandoned your dream?

Was there an event of some kind during your early years that you feel created the inner you that you have become?

CHAPTER THREE:
The Warm Up
These Exercises Can Change Your Life

These exercises, given your full attention, have within them the potential to unlock your "stuck" and get you moving in a productive direction again, focused, unstuck, and back in action.

These exercises will take you through a series of important stages, from planting the seeds, to nurturing their growth, and finally harvesting their bounty. Seeds from one harvest give life to the next harvest – with the proper nurturing. As with growing any crop, the first step must be to prepare the soil.

With that in mind, let me walk you through the preliminary work. Please take all the time you need to answer each of the following questions with as much detail as possible:

1. Are you currently feeling stuck? This may seem obvious, but I'd like you to sit with your answer before writing one single word. Feel it in your bones. What is being stuck doing to your emotions? How and where do you feel it in your body? Is this really how you want to feel about yourself and your life?

2. What is being stuck doing to your life right now? What does it keep you from doing? How does it keep you safe or protected?

3. How have you tried to solve this problem in the past? Why did it fail?

4. What, if any, steps are you planning to take to solve this problem now?

5. Which step(s) in your plan do you think will be the easiest for you to follow? The hardest?

6. What obstacles do you think you will encounter as you begin to solve this problem?

7. Who else can help you overcome these obstacles? What additional internal and external resources will you need?

8. As you go through these steps, how are you going to keep track of your progress as you implement the solution?

9. How will you know when you have solved this problem? How will others know that you have solved your problem? What will you look and act like once your problem is solved?

10. How are you going to celebrate once your problem is solved?

That was the warm-up. All athletes know that the warm-up prepares you for the exercise. Answering the preceding questions was tilling the soil in preparation for what follows: The five questions that can provoke you to get your Self focused, unstuck and back in action. I hope you took the warm-up seriously; it is an essential part of becoming unstuck.

CHAPTER FOUR:
The Exercise That Can
Change Your Life
Ready, Set, GO

Five Simple Exercises to Help You Get Focused, Unstuck and Back in Action.

The following assignment consists of five detailed, thought-provoking questions. Addressing these questions requires careful thought and consideration. Remember, the effort you put into these exercises will determine the quality of your results. Do you want to get unstuck? Then focus on the work and take the action. See? The first step towards being focused, unstuck and back in action is a process that engages your focus, unsticks you a little, and demands action.

First Exercise: Define what you want and what will get you back in action.

In the next five years, what do you want to achieve in your life?

Note: Please remember to have paper and a pen nearby to write down your answers to the exercises. This will make the exercises more effective and you will have record of your thoughts and feeling.

After you have defined what you want your life to be in the next five years, Please write one goal for each year, in the order of their importance. Please take the time to explain in detail what you want to accomplish first in the space above. Here are a few ideas: If it's an increase in income, how do your goals translate into actual dollars and cents? Start in your current year and decide what your monetary goal is for the same time one year from now. You may find this challenging because we all know the difference between reality and fantasy. A fantasy goal is one that defies reason such as attempting to turn the clock back several years. Until science makes that achievable, going back in time is simply a day dream. It is often necessary to make a few sacrifices to achieve to your goal. Look towards the future with the knowledge that you are in control of your life. If you are in a dead end job, what can you do to work towards a promotion or a change in your current position? If your problem lies in the area of relationships, define what your ideal relationship would be and what you can do create harmony and love in your life. Please be as realistic as possible.

Take your time answering this. Think it through, imagining in your mind, living, feeling and experiencing the achievement. Remember discovering what you really want and how to achieve it is the key.

Year One:
Date

Year two:
Date

Year three:
Date

Year four:
Date

Year five:
Date

Second Exercise: Raise Your Awareness.
Are your thoughts stopping you in your tracks?

Write down the major thoughts that come to mind over the course of a couple of days. Doing this on a weekend is ideal. Categorize them by morning, midday and evening thoughts, and then sort them according to whether they are happy thoughts or dark visions of unpleasant scenarios.

This method will help you become aware of how often negative thoughts, fears, and self-talk creep into your mind. Use this awareness to your advantage. When you are aware of a negative thought coming up, replace it with positive thoughts, faith in yourself, and a supportive inner voice. This is an extremely important skill to develop.

Here is a scenario of negative thinking that I have allowed to cloud my thoughts. After I've created a drawing, I review it and usually I feel rather good about it initially. Than after a short period of time I begin to doubt myself. My inner voice tells me it is not good enough. I realize that this little negative voice is my own self-doubt whispering in my ear. We should all be the very best we can be, however sometimes we create negativity simply out of the fear of rejection. When this happens I change the direction of my thoughts. Changing your inner negative self-talk from dark "what if " and "what if I fail" to a positive thought such as " I'm proud of what I created" is a method that works when practiced on a regular bases. You will be surprised when you count the number of bad thoughts you have verses uplifting powerful affirmations. Remember accepting yourself is like building a house and with a good foundation each brick will help that house become sturdier.

Third Exercise: Happiness Check. We only have one life-why waste it?

Pinpoint a source of happiness each day. Pinpoint a source of unhappiness, as well. Write down a description of a happy activity, as well as an unhappy activity. Carefully examine what you were doing at the time you felt good or bad.

Were you at work or at home when you felt at your best?

What activity were you doing at the time you felt the best?

Ask yourself how you can increase that positive experience in your life? Write down a plan of implementation.

How can you incorporate more of the uplifting activity into your life?

Please explain in detail.

Explore what it is that makes you feel unhappy. What are you doing at the particular time you feel badly and examine how you can eliminate and cut down on that activity?

What plan can you implement to totally eliminate the source of unhappiness altogether?

Fourth Exercise: Assess your self-esteem. If you don't believe in yourself, how will you get unstuck and back in action?

Based on your sense of self-worth, what do you think you deserve to achieve? Be honest, and then write it down. Now, bump it up.

WHAT makes you special? Don't be intimidated to sing your own praises. Write down all your talents. Each and every one of us is special. Who are you?

Where do you see room for improvement in your personal development? Describe what you believe are your weak areas. For example, if you are lacking organizational skills, how does that make you feel and what can you do to correct the issue?

If your self-worth was higher, what then do you think you deserve to achieve?

What are you good at and what makes you special? Each of us has skills that we develop because we are passionate about something. For example do you love to cook? Do you feel that cooking is your passion? Well, how can you use that hobby or skill to your happiness advantage?

Do you self-talk yourself out of success? What are your self-doubts?

Please take the time to explain in detail. For example, some people fear failure while others fear success. Both of these emotions and self-talk can become an area which creates procrastination and the awful sensation of being stuck.

Do you have more good "what if" thoughts or negative "what if" thoughts? Take the time to figure it out. It can make a big difference as you begin to become unstuck.

List the good "what if's'- go ahead- the sky is the limit.

List the negative "what if's" – once you list your doom and gloom visions, it becomes easier to see where your fears originate.

If your negative thoughts out weigh positive thoughts practice focusing on only the good thoughts. Thinking negatively is a BAD habit, which you can learn to change. No one can have two thoughts at the same time.

This is not as difficult as it may seem. Keep a small notepad with you at all times. Each time dark thoughts enter your head; take a moment to keep a running total. Simply keep a line count for each of the two categories. At the end of just one week, you will not only be aware of what you are thinking, you will also beware of how to erase a negative thought with a positive one. Awareness is the key. Here are three more great ways to challenge negative thoughts:

1. Ask yourself who's voice the negative thought is in? Yours? Your parents? A teacher?

2. Ask yourself if the negative thought is a useful thought or a destructive thought?

3. Each time you have a negative thought ask yourself if it is true – what evidence do you have that it is?

Fifth Exercise: Are You Willing to Work?

How hard are you willing to work to achieve your goals? Write out a detailed plan for each one of the five years and goals you focused on in the first exercise, one year at a time. The details will make the difference between being stuck in your dreams and "unsticking" yourself.

First plan of action: Check off each detail of your plan when you achieve the goal.

A plan of action counts.

List how you first plan to achieve goal number one. If the rest seem overwhelming, work on the goals as you move through the years. Always remember to date the goals and when you achieve them.

Plan of action year one:
Date:

Plan of action year two:
Date:

Plan of action year three:
Date:

Plan of action year four:
Date:

Plan of action year five:
Date:

Review the plan weekly and access your progress. Choose one special day and time each week. This exercise is vitally important to your success. Actions will create the results you are looking for. The results encourage more enthusiasm and passion.

THIS IS IMPORTANT!!!!!

How do you plan to reward your success as you begin to move forward?

What will you gift yourself when you achieve short term goals? Mid term goals? Your first year goal?

Be proud and be generous with yourself. You will have earned your rewards.

Regular refreshment is a critical component to getting back in action

Review the questions and answers in your workbook on a regular basis.

Read your answers every Monday morning or a day of your choice. Read them out loud in a peaceful place. This verbal reinforcement of defining what you want will raise your awareness, clarify your level of happiness, and assess your self-esteem. Remember your own cooperation and willingness to work in your own behalf will help you remain focused on what you want and recognize any necessary changes you need to make in your life.

When you read your heartfelt answers out loud repeatedly, you will hear your voice making positive statements. This outer voice will replace the negative inner voice, if you let it. This weekly practice will also help you memorize each of your answers naturally, which will translate into a higher comfort level when you take the action your answers dictate.

Now that's what I call a labor of love

The first time I approached these exercises, I struggled. In the end, I had created for myself a very clear plan to follow and an equally clear idea of what I really wanted. For the first time, I was able to focus on what I needed to do in order to get unstuck. With these exercises, I gave myself a detailed plan of action to get moving in a positive direction.

Expect to find this task difficult, and be all right with that. If it feels like work, that's a good sign that it's working. It is time to stop wondering where you are going to start, and simply get started. This workbook is the key to turning your life on. Procrastination is the enemy; it will only get you where you are now, and that is the last thing you want.

You may experience a little brain pain when you start to use those sluggish brain muscles, but believe me, it will be well worth the effort. All you have to do is fill out the workbook, be honest and use a little creativity. If you're doing it right, it will be like discovering a treasure map that leads to a hidden gold mine.

Life still throws me curve balls, some of them big enough to stop me in my tracks, but none of them big enough to get me "stuck" for more than the time it takes to recognize what's happening and do the work to get me "unstuck" and back to moving forward.

May you have the same experience, and carry it forward with you throughout a life of abundant joy created for you, by you.

Myra Goldick

SPECIAL OFFERS
FOR READERS OF THIS BOOK:
Receive a FREE copy of my chapter in
"Mastering the Art of Success"

In this chapter I share my personal thoughts on how to attract success and prosperity into your life. I was honored to share my experience in this intriguing book with amazing people such as Mark Victor Hansen, Jack Canfield, Les Brown and many other successful associates. Within the pages of "Mastering the Art of Success" you will discover valuable insight and direction from top personal development experts to help you create a successful personal and professional life. And you can get my chapter Free right now!

Simply go to my web site at **http://myragoldick.com**. Here you can also sign up for my **FREE** newsletter about our amazing guests on our two internet radio shows, "Never Say Impossible Radio" and "Dancing on our Disabilities". Find out how our guests can help change your life.

Would you like to be a guest on Myra's radio show?

Are you our next guest? Do you have an amazing success story? Do have information that can enrich the lives of others? Simply visit the contact page at http://myragoldick.com and submit your amazing story. If youstory meets the requirements you will receive a free 30 minute interview on either "Never Say Impossible Radio" or "Dancing On Our Disabilities Radio" depending on your genre. This is an amazing opportunity to increase your online visibility, become a media magnet, and share your story with the world.

Remember you are special! You deserve to be happy!

ABOUT THE AUTHOR

Myra Goldick overcame a childhood laced with racial discrimination, poverty and disability during the 50's in New York City. As a child completely paralyzed by polio, Myra was told she would never walk again, and living with it was her only option. After many struggles, several treatments and surgeries, her thinking became clouded by negative emotions and laced with feelings of self-deprivation and self pity. After hitting rock bottom, she slowly began to recognize her own self-worth. Myra decided to fight for her physical and emotional survival. Rejecting the concept that she had limitations was the first step. Through passion, perseverance, and artistic creativity, she rose above adversity and developed a life full of love, success, accomplishment and prosperity

Myra spent 20 years in middle management in cosmetic corporate America. After developing post-polio syndrome, she left the cosmetic industry and retrained as a millinery designer. She enjoyed 8 more years as a successful hat designer on 7th Avenue, in New York City.

Today Myra is an author, speaker, professional artist, and the host of the Never Say Impossible and Dancing On Our Disabilities Internet radio shows. Her mission is to motivate, inspire, and inform her audience through the ancient art of verbal communication. One person's path to success, when shared with others, can become a method of prosperity for mankind.

Myra says, "The key to overcoming the hard times and succeeding beyond ordinary expectations is to recognize that anything is possible, if you believe it is."

The *Never Say Impossible Show* focuses on healthcare, story telling, spirituality, and business trends, while offering great entertainment at the same time. For more information visit http://www.myragoldick.com/never-say-impossible-2/#

The Dancing On Our Disabilities Show is a forum created to share medical information, inspiring motivational and amazing personal stories of how to live with disabilities and still create a successful life. The show covers everything from Autism to Traumatic Brain Injury. Myra is the founder of Living Through Art, Inc. whose mission is to share information and creativity through a variety of resources and individuals for the purpose of improving the quality of life for everyone. For more information visit: **http://www.myragoldick.com**

Please contact Myra for further information about her products and services:

email: myra@myragoldick.com
http://www.myragoldick.com
http://www.myrasart.com
http://www.myra-goldick,artisteebsites.com
http://facebook.com/neversayimpossibleradio
http://facebook.com/dancing-on-our-disabilities
http://youtube.com/user/myrasart

ACKNOWLEDGEMENTS

I extend gratitude to my business coach John C Robinson whose expertise, skill and professionalism has guided me through the development of this workbook. I would also like to extend a special thank you to Howard VanEs, President of Let's Write Books, Inc. who has helped me package and publish this book.

A FINAL WORD

Creativity and the expression of that creativity has been a very important part of my healing journey. On this page and the next I have shared some of my paintings. If you would like to see more paintings please visit my web page **http://www.myrasart.com.**

FOCUSED, UNSTUCK, and BACK IN ACTION
Workbook by Myra Goldick

The One Key YOU Can Use To Restart Your Engine Whenever Life Grinds You to a Halt.
Stop Procrastinating — Find out how to Reinvent Yourself Today!

Focused Unstuck, and Back in Action eBook/Workbook can help change your life!
- You will be amazed how quickly your life is going to change
- You will begin creating new rewards and success in your life
- You will rediscover your passion and joy
- Your life will have new meaning and purpose

Create your very own guide to discovering your real mission in life!

I am overjoyed to share with you the key I use to restart my engine when life grinds me to a halt. It can be your magic key today. Reinventing yourself is easier than you think. Getting unstuck is only a click away; take action today.

Visit http://myragoldick.Com/Available on Amazon
Check out my newest book-

"Dancing on your Disabilities-Never Say Impossible to your Dreams"
A guide to happiness no matter what!

Sign up for my Never Say Impossible Talk Show announcements and get a free chapter in Mastering the Art of Success
Review
"I've read this book multiple times and I keep reading it because it is so applicable to our lives in the 21st century. Regardless of the success you've had, the ambitions you harbor, or any failures you may have experienced in the past, Myra's work is at once inspirational, practical, and achievable. With "Focused, Unstuck, and Back in Action", every one of us can become more focused and return to our goals with more energy than ever before ... I believe this book can help anyone achieve greater results."
John Robinson- Master Business Caoch